Podcast Planner

INFORMATIONS

NAME

ADDRESS

E-MAIL ADDRESS

WEBSITE

PHONE   FAX

EMERGENCY CONTACT PERSON

PHONE   FAX

9 Tips for Improving My Podcast

1. **Create a podcast template.** You can easily improve your workflow by creating a template for each podcast episode. The template should determine the podcast format and include pre-recorded podcast intros and outros. To help set expectations for the listener, the best podcasts introduce the template starting with the first episode. You can always introduce or explore new templates for your podcast, but consider maintaining the same template for each season to avoid a jarring experience for the listener.

2. **Improve your audio quality with the right recording equipment.** The right podcast equipment can help improve your sound quality by making your audio clearer, less harsh, and more reliable. Whether you're recording your podcast with in-person interviewees, with another podcast host, or over Zoom or Skype, having the right equipment can help improve the audio quality. Instead of using the built-in microphone on your device, consider purchasing a USB microphone with a pop filter. Starting with high-quality audio has the added benefit of making the podcast editing process easier later on.

3. **Record in a quiet environment.** Studios provide the best environment for podcast recording, but a small, quiet room such as a closet can work well for at-home recording. Small spaces with soft surfaces reduce the potential for background noise and echoes that could make your audio sound messy.

4. **Explore free recording and editing software first.** There are several audio editing and recording software options available on the market, making it easy to find software that will work for you. Most entry-level recording software (such as GarageBand or Audacity) is free and suitable for the needs of first-time podcasters. If you're looking to have more control over the editing process or need specific sound effects, consider purchasing plug-ins before buying entirely new software.

5. **Include intro music.** Set the right tone for your podcast by kicking off each episode with intro music. You could record your own, hire a musician, or use royalty-free music that can be found for free online.

6. **Include eye-catching cover art.** Podcast cover art is the first thing potential listeners will see while scrolling through podcast directories. Be sure that your cover art includes your podcast name and gives new listeners an idea of what your show is about.

7. **Include helpful show notes.** Show notes appear alongside the podcast episode. Show notes can contain a transcription of the audio, helpful links, credits, or a brief description of the episode.

8. **Promote your podcast by publishing supporting materials online.** Promote your podcast by creating a podcast website. Blogging about new episodes and related topics you're passionate about is a great way to engage new podcast listeners and improve your search engine optimization, or SEO. SEO helps position your website on search results pages and is one of the best tools for capturing potential new subscribers. An established website can also help support future monetization efforts like sponsored content or podcast merchandise.

9. **Publish your podcast on multiple hosting platforms.** There are several popular podcast hosting services that will host your podcast at no cost. Making your podcast as widely available as possible will help broaden your audience.

Podcast name

....

| **EPISODE #** | **TOPIC TO DISCUSS** |

RECORDING DATE

....
....
....
PUBLISHING DATE
....
....
....
RECORDING LOCATION
....

HOSTS	**GUESTS**	**LENGTH**

MAIN GOAL FOR THIS PODCAST

....
....
....
....

CONTEST

SPONSOR ....
PRIZE ....
WINNER ....

TALKING POINTS

....
....
....
....
....
....

Podcast Review

THINGS I NEED TO PRACTICE

....
....
....
....

THINGS I REALLY ENJOYED :)

....
....
....
....

THINGS I DIDN'T EXPECTED

....
....
....
....

BUSINESS / PROMOTION

....
....
....
....
....
....

NOTES

....
....
....
....
....
....

Podcast Rating ☆ ☆ ☆ ☆ ☆

Podcast name ....

EPISODE #

RECORDING DATE

PUBLISHING DATE

RECORDING LOCATION

TOPIC TO DISCUSS

....
....
....
....
....
....
....

HOSTS

GUESTS

LENGTH

MAIN GOAL FOR THIS PODCAST

....
....
....
....

CONTEST

SPONSOR ....
PRIZE ....
WINNER ....

TALKING POINTS

....
....
....
....
....
....

Podcast Review

THINGS I NEED TO PRACTICE

....
....
....
....

THINGS I REALLY ENJOYED :)

....
....
....
....

THINGS I DIDN'T EXPECTED

....
....
....
....

BUSINESS / PROMOTION

....
....
....
....
....
....

NOTES

....
....
....
....
....
....

Podcast Rating ☆ ☆ ☆ ☆ ☆

Podcast name

EPISODE #

RECORDING DATE

PUBLISHING DATE

RECORDING LOCATION

TOPIC TO DISCUSS

HOSTS

GUESTS

LENGTH

MAIN GOAL FOR THIS PODCAST

CONTEST

SPONSOR

PRIZE

WINNER

TALKING POINTS

Podcast Review

THINGS I NEED TO PRACTICE

THINGS I REALLY ENJOYED :)

THINGS I DIDN'T EXPECTED

BUSINESS / PROMOTION

NOTES

Podcast Rating ⭐ ⭐ ⭐ ⭐ ⭐

Podcast name

....

EPISODE #

RECORDING DATE

PUBLISHING DATE

RECORDING LOCATION

TOPIC TO DISCUSS

....
....
....
....
....
....
....

HOSTS	GUESTS	LENGTH

MAIN GOAL FOR THIS PODCAST

....
....
....
....

CONTEST

SPONSOR ....
PRIZE ....
WINNER ....

TALKING POINTS

....
....
....
....
....
....

Podcast Review

THINGS I NEED TO PRACTICE

THINGS I REALLY ENJOYED :)

THINGS I DIDN'T EXPECTED

BUSINESS / PROMOTION

NOTES

Podcast Rating ☆ ☆ ☆ ☆ ☆

Podcast name ....

EPISODE

RECORDING DATE

PUBLISHING DATE

RECORDING LOCATION

TOPIC TO DISCUSS

....
....
....
....
....
....
....

HOSTS

GUESTS

LENGTH

MAIN GOAL FOR THIS PODCAST

....
....
....
....

CONTEST

SPONSOR ....
PRIZE ....
WINNER ....

TALKING POINTS

....
....
....
....
....
....

Podcast Review

THINGS I NEED TO PRACTICE

THINGS I REALLY ENJOYED :)

THINGS I DIDN'T EXPECTED

BUSINESS / PROMOTION

NOTES

Podcast Rating ⭐ ⭐ ⭐ ⭐ ⭐

Podcast name

....

EPISODE #

RECORDING DATE

PUBLISHING DATE

RECORDING LOCATION

TOPIC TO DISCUSS

....
....
....
....
....
....
....

HOSTS

GUESTS

LENGTH

MAIN GOAL FOR THIS PODCAST

....
....
....
....

CONTEST

SPONSOR ....

PRIZE ....

WINNER ....

TALKING POINTS

....
....
....
....
....
....

Podcast Review

THINGS I NEED TO PRACTICE

THINGS I REALLY ENJOYED :)

THINGS I DIDN'T EXPECTED

BUSINESS / PROMOTION

NOTES

Podcast Rating

Podcast name

....

EPISODE #

RECORDING DATE

PUBLISHING DATE

RECORDING LOCATION

TOPIC TO DISCUSS

....
....
....
....
....
....
....

HOSTS

GUESTS

LENGTH

MAIN GOAL FOR THIS PODCAST

....
....
....
....

CONTEST

SPONSOR ....
PRIZE ....
WINNER ....

TALKING POINTS

....
....
....
....
....
....

Podcast Review

THINGS I NEED TO PRACTICE

THINGS I REALLY ENJOYED :)

THINGS I DIDN'T EXPECTED

BUSINESS / PROMOTION

NOTES

Podcast Rating ⭐ ⭐ ⭐ ⭐ ⭐

Podcast name ....

EPISODE #

RECORDING DATE

PUBLISHING DATE

RECORDING LOCATION

TOPIC TO DISCUSS

....
....
....
....
....
....
....

HOSTS

GUESTS

LENGTH

MAIN GOAL FOR THIS PODCAST

....
....
....
....

CONTEST

SPONSOR ....
PRIZE ....
WINNER ....

TALKING POINTS

....
....
....
....
....
....

Podcast Review

THINGS I NEED TO PRACTICE

THINGS I REALLY ENJOYED :)

THINGS I DIDN'T EXPECTED

BUSINESS / PROMOTION

NOTES

Podcast Rating ☆ ☆ ☆ ☆ ☆

Podcast name

....

EPISODE #

RECORDING DATE

PUBLISHING DATE

RECORDING LOCATION

TOPIC TO DISCUSS

....
....
....
....
....
....
....

HOSTS	GUESTS	LENGTH

MAIN GOAL FOR THIS PODCAST

....
....
....
....

CONTEST

SPONSOR ....
PRIZE ....
WINNER ....

TALKING POINTS

....
....
....
....
....
....

Podcast Review

THINGS I NEED TO PRACTICE

THINGS I REALLY ENJOYED :)

THINGS I DIDN'T EXPECTED

BUSINESS / PROMOTION

NOTES

Podcast Rating ☆ ☆ ☆ ☆ ☆

Podcast name

....

EPISODE #

RECORDING DATE

PUBLISHING DATE

RECORDING LOCATION

TOPIC TO DISCUSS

....
....
....
....
....
....
....

HOSTS

GUESTS

LENGTH

MAIN GOAL FOR THIS PODCAST

....
....
....
....

CONTEST

SPONSOR ....
PRIZE ....
WINNER ....

TALKING POINTS

....
....
....
....
....
....

Podcast Review

THINGS I NEED TO PRACTICE

....
....
....
....

THINGS I REALLY ENJOYED :)

....
....
....
....

THINGS I DIDN'T EXPECTED

....
....
....
....

BUSINESS / PROMOTION

....
....
....
....
....

NOTES

....
....
....
....
....

Podcast Rating ☆ ☆ ☆ ☆ ☆

Podcast name

....

EPISODE #

RECORDING DATE

PUBLISHING DATE

RECORDING LOCATION

TOPIC TO DISCUSS

....
....
....
....
....
....
....

HOSTS

GUESTS

LENGTH

MAIN GOAL FOR THIS PODCAST

....
....
....
....

CONTEST

SPONSOR ....
PRIZE ....
WINNER ....

TALKING POINTS

....
....
....
....
....
....

Podcast Review

THINGS I NEED TO PRACTICE

....
....
....
....

THINGS I REALLY ENJOYED :)

....
....
....
....

THINGS I DIDN'T EXPECTED

....
....
....
....

BUSINESS / PROMOTION

....
....
....
....
....
....

NOTES

....
....
....
....
....

Podcast Rating ☆ ☆ ☆ ☆ ☆

Podcast name

....

EPISODE #

RECORDING DATE

PUBLISHING DATE

RECORDING LOCATION

TOPIC TO DISCUSS

....
....
....
....
....
....
....

HOSTS

GUESTS

LENGTH

MAIN GOAL FOR THIS PODCAST

....
....
....
....

CONTEST

SPONSOR ....
PRIZE ....
WINNER ....

TALKING POINTS

....
....
....
....
....
....

Podcast Review

THINGS I NEED TO PRACTICE

THINGS I REALLY ENJOYED :)

THINGS I DIDN'T EXPECTED

BUSINESS / PROMOTION

NOTES

Podcast Rating ☆ ☆ ☆ ☆ ☆

Podcast name

....

EPISODE #

RECORDING DATE

PUBLISHING DATE

RECORDING LOCATION

TOPIC TO DISCUSS

....
....
....
....
....
....
....

HOSTS

GUESTS

LENGTH

MAIN GOAL FOR THIS PODCAST

....
....
....
....

CONTEST

SPONSOR ....
PRIZE ....
WINNER ....

TALKING POINTS

....
....
....
....
....
....

Podcast Review

THINGS I NEED TO PRACTICE

THINGS I REALLY ENJOYED :)

THINGS I DIDN'T EXPECTED

BUSINESS / PROMOTION

NOTES

Podcast Rating ⭐ ⭐ ⭐ ⭐ ⭐

Podcast name

....

EPISODE #

RECORDING DATE

PUBLISHING DATE

RECORDING LOCATION

TOPIC TO DISCUSS

....
....
....
....
....
....
....

HOSTS

GUESTS

LENGTH

MAIN GOAL FOR THIS PODCAST

....
....
....
....

CONTEST

SPONSOR ....
PRIZE ....
WINNER ....

TALKING POINTS

....
....
....
....
....
....

Podcast Review

THINGS I NEED TO PRACTICE

THINGS I REALLY ENJOYED :)

THINGS I DIDN'T EXPECTED

BUSINESS / PROMOTION

NOTES

Podcast Rating ☆ ☆ ☆ ☆ ☆

Podcast name

....

EPISODE #

RECORDING DATE

PUBLISHING DATE

RECORDING LOCATION

TOPIC TO DISCUSS

....
....
....
....
....
....
....

HOSTS

GUESTS

LENGTH

MAIN GOAL FOR THIS PODCAST

....
....
....
....

CONTEST

SPONSOR ....
PRIZE ....
WINNER ....

TALKING POINTS

....
....
....
....
....
....

Podcast Review

THINGS I NEED TO PRACTICE

....
....
....
....

THINGS I REALLY ENJOYED :)

....
....
....
....

THINGS I DIDN'T EXPECTED

....
....
....
....

BUSINESS / PROMOTION

....
....
....
....
....
....

NOTES

....
....
....
....
....
....

Podcast Rating

Podcast name

....

EPISODE #

RECORDING DATE

PUBLISHING DATE

RECORDING LOCATION

TOPIC TO DISCUSS

....
....
....
....
....
....
....

HOSTS

GUESTS

LENGTH

MAIN GOAL FOR THIS PODCAST

....
....
....
....

CONTEST

SPONSOR ....
PRIZE ....
WINNER ....

TALKING POINTS

....
....
....
....
....
....

Podcast Review

THINGS I NEED TO PRACTICE

....
....
....
....

THINGS I REALLY ENJOYED :)

....
....
....
....

THINGS I DIDN'T EXPECTED

....
....
....
....

BUSINESS / PROMOTION

....
....
....
....
....
....

NOTES

....
....
....
....
....

Podcast Rating ☆ ☆ ☆ ☆ ☆

Podcast name

....

EPISODE #

RECORDING DATE

PUBLISHING DATE

RECORDING LOCATION

TOPIC TO DISCUSS

....
....
....
....
....
....
....

HOSTS	GUESTS	LENGTH

MAIN GOAL FOR THIS PODCAST

....
....
....
....

CONTEST

SPONSOR ....

PRIZE ....

WINNER ....

TALKING POINTS

....
....
....
....
....
....

Podcast Review

THINGS I NEED TO PRACTICE

....
....
....
....

THINGS I REALLY ENJOYED :)

....
....
....
....

THINGS I DIDN'T EXPECTED

....
....
....
....

BUSINESS / PROMOTION

....
....
....
....
....
....

NOTES

....
....
....
....
....

Podcast Rating ⭐ ⭐ ⭐ ⭐ ⭐

Podcast name

....

EPISODE

RECORDING DATE

PUBLISHING DATE

RECORDING LOCATION

TOPIC TO DISCUSS

....
....
....
....
....
....
....

HOSTS

GUESTS

LENGTH

MAIN GOAL FOR THIS PODCAST

....
....
....
....

CONTEST

SPONSOR ....
PRIZE ....
WINNER ....

TALKING POINTS

....
....
....
....
....
....

Podcast Review

THINGS I NEED TO PRACTICE

THINGS I REALLY ENJOYED :)

THINGS I DIDN'T EXPECTED

BUSINESS / PROMOTION

NOTES

Podcast Rating ☆ ☆ ☆ ☆ ☆

Podcast name

....

EPISODE #

RECORDING DATE

PUBLISHING DATE

RECORDING LOCATION

TOPIC TO DISCUSS

....
....
....
....
....
....
....

HOSTS

GUESTS

LENGTH

MAIN GOAL FOR THIS PODCAST

....
....
....
....

CONTEST

SPONSOR ....
PRIZE ....
WINNER ....

TALKING POINTS

....
....
....
....
....
....

Podcast Review

THINGS I NEED TO PRACTICE

THINGS I REALLY ENJOYED :)

THINGS I DIDN'T EXPECTED

BUSINESS / PROMOTION

NOTES

Podcast Rating ☆ ☆ ☆ ☆ ☆

Podcast name

....

EPISODE #

RECORDING DATE

PUBLISHING DATE

RECORDING LOCATION

TOPIC TO DISCUSS

....
....
....
....
....
....
....

HOSTS	GUESTS	LENGTH

MAIN GOAL FOR THIS PODCAST

....
....
....
....

CONTEST

SPONSOR ....
PRIZE ....
WINNER ....

TALKING POINTS

....
....
....
....
....
....

Podcast Review

THINGS I NEED TO PRACTICE

THINGS I REALLY ENJOYED :)

THINGS I DIDN'T EXPECTED

BUSINESS / PROMOTION

NOTES

Podcast Rating

⭐ ⭐ ⭐ ⭐ ⭐

Podcast name

EPISODE

RECORDING DATE

PUBLISHING DATE

RECORDING LOCATION

TOPIC TO DISCUSS

HOSTS

GUESTS

LENGTH

MAIN GOAL FOR THIS PODCAST

CONTEST

SPONSOR

PRIZE

WINNER

TALKING POINTS

Podcast Review

THINGS I NEED TO PRACTICE

THINGS I REALLY ENJOYED :)

THINGS I DIDN'T EXPECTED

BUSINESS / PROMOTION

NOTES

Podcast Rating

Podcast name

....

EPISODE #

RECORDING DATE

PUBLISHING DATE

RECORDING LOCATION

TOPIC TO DISCUSS

....
....
....
....
....
....
....

HOSTS	**GUESTS**	**LENGTH**

MAIN GOAL FOR THIS PODCAST

....
....
....
....

CONTEST

SPONSOR ....
PRIZE ....
WINNER ....

TALKING POINTS

....
....
....
....
....
....

Podcast Review

THINGS I NEED TO PRACTICE

THINGS I REALLY ENJOYED :)

THINGS I DIDN'T EXPECTED

BUSINESS / PROMOTION

NOTES

Podcast Rating

Podcast name

EPISODE #

RECORDING DATE

PUBLISHING DATE

RECORDING LOCATION

TOPIC TO DISCUSS

HOSTS	GUESTS	LENGTH

MAIN GOAL FOR THIS PODCAST

CONTEST

SPONSOR

PRIZE

WINNER

TALKING POINTS

Podcast Review

THINGS I NEED TO PRACTICE

....
....
....
....

THINGS I REALLY ENJOYED :)

....
....
....
....

THINGS I DIDN'T EXPECTED

....
....
....
....

BUSINESS / PROMOTION

....
....
....
....
....
....

NOTES

....
....
....
....
....
....

Podcast Rating   ☆ ☆ ☆ ☆ ☆

Podcast name

....

EPISODE #

RECORDING DATE

PUBLISHING DATE

RECORDING LOCATION

TOPIC TO DISCUSS

....
....
....
....
....
....
....

HOSTS

GUESTS

LENGTH

MAIN GOAL FOR THIS PODCAST

....
....
....
....

CONTEST

SPONSOR ....
PRIZE ....
WINNER ....

TALKING POINTS

....
....
....
....
....
....

Podcast Review

THINGS I NEED TO PRACTICE

THINGS I REALLY ENJOYED :)

THINGS I DIDN'T EXPECTED

BUSINESS / PROMOTION

NOTES

Podcast Rating ⭐ ⭐ ⭐ ⭐ ⭐

Podcast name

....

EPISODE #

RECORDING DATE

PUBLISHING DATE

RECORDING LOCATION

TOPIC TO DISCUSS

....
....
....
....
....
....
....

HOSTS

GUESTS

LENGTH

MAIN GOAL FOR THIS PODCAST

....
....
....
....

CONTEST

SPONSOR ....
PRIZE ....
WINNER ....

TALKING POINTS

....
....
....
....
....
....

Podcast Review

THINGS I NEED TO PRACTICE

THINGS I REALLY ENJOYED :)

THINGS I DIDN'T EXPECTED

BUSINESS / PROMOTION

NOTES

Podcast Rating ☆ ☆ ☆ ☆ ☆

Podcast name

....

EPISODE #

RECORDING DATE

PUBLISHING DATE

RECORDING LOCATION

TOPIC TO DISCUSS

....
....
....
....
....
....
....

HOSTS

GUESTS

LENGTH

MAIN GOAL FOR THIS PODCAST

....
....
....
....

CONTEST

SPONSOR ....
PRIZE ....
WINNER ....

TALKING POINTS

....
....
....
....
....
....

Podcast Review

THINGS I NEED TO PRACTICE

....
....
....
....

THINGS I REALLY ENJOYED :)

....
....
....
....

THINGS I DIDN'T EXPECTED

....
....
....
....

BUSINESS / PROMOTION

....
....
....
....
....

NOTES

....
....
....
....
....
....

Podcast Rating ☆ ☆ ☆ ☆ ☆

Podcast name

....

EPISODE

RECORDING DATE

PUBLISHING DATE

RECORDING LOCATION

TOPIC TO DISCUSS

....
....
....
....
....
....
....

HOSTS

GUESTS

LENGTH

MAIN GOAL FOR THIS PODCAST

....
....
....
....

CONTEST

SPONSOR ....
PRIZE ....
WINNER ....

TALKING POINTS

....
....
....
....
....
....

Podcast Review

THINGS I NEED TO PRACTICE

....
....
....
....

THINGS I REALLY ENJOYED :)

....
....
....
....

THINGS I DIDN'T EXPECTED

....
....
....
....

BUSINESS / PROMOTION

....
....
....
....
....
....

NOTES

....
....
....
....
....
....

Podcast Rating ☆ ☆ ☆ ☆ ☆

Podcast name

....

EPISODE #

RECORDING DATE

PUBLISHING DATE

RECORDING LOCATION

TOPIC TO DISCUSS

....
....
....
....
....
....
....

HOSTS

GUESTS

LENGTH

MAIN GOAL FOR THIS PODCAST

....
....
....
....

CONTEST

SPONSOR ....
PRIZE ....
WINNER ....

TALKING POINTS

....
....
....
....
....
....

Podcast Review

THINGS I NEED TO PRACTICE

THINGS I REALLY ENJOYED :)

THINGS I DIDN'T EXPECTED

BUSINESS / PROMOTION

NOTES

Podcast Rating ⭐ ⭐ ⭐ ⭐ ⭐

Podcast name

EPISODE

RECORDING DATE

PUBLISHING DATE

RECORDING LOCATION

TOPIC TO DISCUSS

HOSTS

GUESTS

LENGTH

MAIN GOAL FOR THIS PODCAST

CONTEST

SPONSOR

PRIZE

WINNER

TALKING POINTS

Podcast Review

THINGS I NEED TO PRACTICE

THINGS I REALLY ENJOYED :)

THINGS I DIDN'T EXPECTED

BUSINESS / PROMOTION

NOTES

Podcast Rating ☆ ☆ ☆ ☆ ☆

Podcast name

....

EPISODE

RECORDING DATE

PUBLISHING DATE

RECORDING LOCATION

TOPIC TO DISCUSS

....
....
....
....
....
....
....

HOSTS

GUESTS

LENGTH

MAIN GOAL FOR THIS PODCAST

....
....
....
....

CONTEST

SPONSOR ....
PRIZE ....
WINNER ....

TALKING POINTS

....
....
....
....
....
....

Podcast Review

THINGS I NEED TO PRACTICE

....
....
....
....

THINGS I REALLY ENJOYED :)

....
....
....
....

THINGS I DIDN'T EXPECTED

....
....
....
....

BUSINESS / PROMOTION

....
....
....
....
....
....

NOTES

....
....
....
....
....
....

Podcast Rating ☆ ☆ ☆ ☆ ☆

Podcast name

....

EPISODE #		TOPIC TO DISCUSS

RECORDING DATE

PUBLISHING DATE

RECORDING LOCATION

TOPIC TO DISCUSS
....
....
....
....
....
....
....

HOSTS	GUESTS	LENGTH

MAIN GOAL FOR THIS PODCAST

....
....
....
....

CONTEST

SPONSOR ....
PRIZE ....
WINNER ....

TALKING POINTS

....
....
....
....
....
....

Podcast Review

THINGS I NEED TO PRACTICE

THINGS I REALLY ENJOYED :)

THINGS I DIDN'T EXPECTED

BUSINESS / PROMOTION

NOTES

Podcast Rating ⭐ ⭐ ⭐ ⭐ ⭐

Podcast name

....

EPISODE #

RECORDING DATE

PUBLISHING DATE

RECORDING LOCATION

TOPIC TO DISCUSS

....
....
....
....
....
....
....

HOSTS

GUESTS

LENGTH

MAIN GOAL FOR THIS PODCAST

....
....
....
....

CONTEST

SPONSOR ....

PRIZE ....

WINNER ....

TALKING POINTS

....
....
....
....
....
....

Podcast Review

THINGS I NEED TO PRACTICE

THINGS I REALLY ENJOYED :)

THINGS I DIDN'T EXPECTED

BUSINESS / PROMOTION

NOTES

Podcast Rating ☆ ☆ ☆ ☆ ☆

Podcast name

....

EPISODE

RECORDING DATE

PUBLISHING DATE

RECORDING LOCATION

TOPIC TO DISCUSS

....
....
....
....
....
....
....

HOSTS

GUESTS

LENGTH

MAIN GOAL FOR THIS PODCAST

....
....
....
....

CONTEST

SPONSOR ....
PRIZE ....
WINNER ....

TALKING POINTS

....
....
....
....
....
....

Podcast Review

THINGS I NEED TO PRACTICE

....
....
....
....

THINGS I REALLY ENJOYED :)

....
....
....
....

THINGS I DIDN'T EXPECTED

....
....
....
....

BUSINESS / PROMOTION

....
....
....
....
....

NOTES

....
....
....
....
....

Podcast Rating

Podcast name

....

EPISODE #

RECORDING DATE

PUBLISHING DATE

RECORDING LOCATION

TOPIC TO DISCUSS

....
....
....
....
....
....
....

HOSTS	**GUESTS**	**LENGTH**

MAIN GOAL FOR THIS PODCAST

....
....
....
....

CONTEST

SPONSOR ....
PRIZE ....
WINNER ....

TALKING POINTS

....
....
....
....
....
....

Podcast Review

THINGS I NEED TO PRACTICE

THINGS I REALLY ENJOYED :)

THINGS I DIDN'T EXPECTED

BUSINESS / PROMOTION

NOTES

Podcast Rating ⭐ ⭐ ⭐ ⭐ ⭐

Podcast name ....

EPISODE

RECORDING DATE

PUBLISHING DATE

RECORDING LOCATION

TOPIC TO DISCUSS

....
....
....
....
....
....
....

HOSTS

GUESTS

LENGTH

MAIN GOAL FOR THIS PODCAST

....
....
....
....

CONTEST

SPONSOR ....
PRIZE ....
WINNER ....

TALKING POINTS

....
....
....
....
....
....

Podcast Review

THINGS I NEED TO PRACTICE

....
....
....
....

THINGS I REALLY ENJOYED :)

....
....
....
....

THINGS I DIDN'T EXPECTED

....
....
....
....

BUSINESS / PROMOTION

....
....
....
....
....
....

NOTES

....
....
....
....
....
....

Podcast Rating   ☆ ☆ ☆ ☆ ☆

Podcast name

....

EPISODE

RECORDING DATE

PUBLISHING DATE

RECORDING LOCATION

TOPIC TO DISCUSS

....
....
....
....
....
....
....

HOSTS

GUESTS

LENGTH

MAIN GOAL FOR THIS PODCAST

....
....
....
....

CONTEST

SPONSOR ....
PRIZE ....
WINNER ....

TALKING POINTS

....
....
....
....
....
....

Podcast Review

THINGS I NEED TO PRACTICE

....
....
....
....

THINGS I REALLY ENJOYED :)

....
....
....
....

THINGS I DIDN'T EXPECTED

....
....
....
....

BUSINESS / PROMOTION

....
....
....
....
....

NOTES

....
....
....
....
....
....

Podcast Rating ★ ★ ★ ★ ★

Podcast name

....

EPISODE #

RECORDING DATE

PUBLISHING DATE

RECORDING LOCATION

TOPIC TO DISCUSS

....
....
....
....
....
....
....
....

HOSTS

GUESTS

LENGTH

MAIN GOAL FOR THIS PODCAST

....
....
....
....

CONTEST

SPONSOR ....
PRIZE ....
WINNER ....

TALKING POINTS

....
....
....
....
....
....

Podcast Review

THINGS I NEED TO PRACTICE

THINGS I REALLY ENJOYED :)

THINGS I DIDN'T EXPECTED

BUSINESS / PROMOTION

NOTES

Podcast Rating ⭐ ⭐ ⭐ ⭐ ⭐

Podcast name

EPISODE #

RECORDING DATE

PUBLISHING DATE

RECORDING LOCATION

TOPIC TO DISCUSS

HOSTS

GUESTS

LENGTH

MAIN GOAL FOR THIS PODCAST

CONTEST

SPONSOR

PRIZE

WINNER

TALKING POINTS

Podcast Review

THINGS I NEED TO PRACTICE

THINGS I REALLY ENJOYED :)

THINGS I DIDN'T EXPECTED

BUSINESS / PROMOTION

NOTES

Podcast Rating ⭐ ⭐ ⭐ ⭐ ⭐

Podcast name

EPISODE

RECORDING DATE

PUBLISHING DATE

RECORDING LOCATION

TOPIC TO DISCUSS

HOSTS

GUESTS

LENGTH

MAIN GOAL FOR THIS PODCAST

CONTEST

SPONSOR

PRIZE

WINNER

TALKING POINTS

Podcast Review

THINGS I NEED TO PRACTICE

....
....
....
....

THINGS I REALLY ENJOYED :)

....
....
....
....

THINGS I DIDN'T EXPECTED

....
....
....
....

BUSINESS / PROMOTION

....
....
....
....
....
....

NOTES

....
....
....
....
....
....

Podcast Rating ☆ ☆ ☆ ☆ ☆

Podcast name

EPISODE

RECORDING DATE

PUBLISHING DATE

RECORDING LOCATION

TOPIC TO DISCUSS

HOSTS

GUESTS

LENGTH

MAIN GOAL FOR THIS PODCAST

CONTEST

SPONSOR

PRIZE

WINNER

TALKING POINTS

Podcast Review

THINGS I NEED TO PRACTICE

THINGS I REALLY ENJOYED :)

THINGS I DIDN'T EXPECTED

BUSINESS / PROMOTION

NOTES

Podcast Rating

Podcast name

EPISODE #

RECORDING DATE

PUBLISHING DATE

RECORDING LOCATION

TOPIC TO DISCUSS

HOSTS

GUESTS

LENGTH

MAIN GOAL FOR THIS PODCAST

CONTEST

SPONSOR

PRIZE

WINNER

TALKING POINTS

Podcast Review

THINGS I NEED TO PRACTICE

THINGS I REALLY ENJOYED :)

THINGS I DIDN'T EXPECTED

BUSINESS / PROMOTION

NOTES

Podcast Rating

Podcast name

....

EPISODE

RECORDING DATE

PUBLISHING DATE

RECORDING LOCATION

TOPIC TO DISCUSS

....
....
....
....
....
....
....

HOSTS

GUESTS

LENGTH

MAIN GOAL FOR THIS PODCAST

....
....
....
....

CONTEST

SPONSOR ....
PRIZE ....
WINNER ....

TALKING POINTS

....
....
....
....
....
....

Podcast Review

THINGS I NEED TO PRACTICE

....
....
....
....

THINGS I REALLY ENJOYED :)

....
....
....
....

THINGS I DIDN'T EXPECTED

....
....
....
....

BUSINESS / PROMOTION

....
....
....
....
....

NOTES

....
....
....
....
....
....

Podcast Rating
★ ★ ★ ★ ★

Podcast name

....

EPISODE #

RECORDING DATE

PUBLISHING DATE

RECORDING LOCATION

TOPIC TO DISCUSS

....
....
....
....
....
....
....

HOSTS

GUESTS

LENGTH

MAIN GOAL FOR THIS PODCAST

....
....
....
....

CONTEST

SPONSOR ....

PRIZE ....

WINNER ....

TALKING POINTS

....
....
....
....
....
....

Podcast Review

THINGS I NEED TO PRACTICE

THINGS I REALLY ENJOYED :)

THINGS I DIDN'T EXPECTED

BUSINESS / PROMOTION

NOTES

Podcast Rating ⭐ ⭐ ⭐ ⭐ ⭐

Podcast name

....

EPISODE #

RECORDING DATE

PUBLISHING DATE

RECORDING LOCATION

TOPIC TO DISCUSS

....
....
....
....
....
....
....

HOSTS	GUESTS	LENGTH

MAIN GOAL FOR THIS PODCAST

....
....
....
....

CONTEST

SPONSOR ....

PRIZE ....

WINNER ....

TALKING POINTS

....
....
....
....
....
....

Podcast Review

THINGS I NEED TO PRACTICE

....
....
....
....

THINGS I REALLY ENJOYED :)

....
....
....
....

THINGS I DIDN'T EXPECTED

....
....
....
....

BUSINESS / PROMOTION

....
....
....
....
....

NOTES

....
....
....
....
....

Podcast Rating ★ ★ ★ ★ ★

Podcast name

....

EPISODE

RECORDING DATE

PUBLISHING DATE

RECORDING LOCATION

TOPIC TO DISCUSS

....
....
....
....
....
....
....

HOSTS

GUESTS

LENGTH

MAIN GOAL FOR THIS PODCAST

....
....
....
....

CONTEST

SPONSOR ....
PRIZE ....
WINNER ....

TALKING POINTS

....
....
....
....
....
....

Podcast Review

THINGS I NEED TO PRACTICE

THINGS I REALLY ENJOYED :)

THINGS I DIDN'T EXPECTED

BUSINESS / PROMOTION

NOTES

Podcast Rating

Podcast name

....

EPISODE #

RECORDING DATE

PUBLISHING DATE

RECORDING LOCATION

TOPIC TO DISCUSS

....
....
....
....
....
....
....

HOSTS

GUESTS

LENGTH

MAIN GOAL FOR THIS PODCAST

....
....
....
....

CONTEST

SPONSOR ....
PRIZE ....
WINNER ....

TALKING POINTS

....
....
....
....
....
....

Podcast Review

THINGS I NEED TO PRACTICE

....
....
....
....

THINGS I REALLY ENJOYED :)

....
....
....
....

THINGS I DIDN'T EXPECTED

....
....
....
....

BUSINESS / PROMOTION

....
....
....
....
....
....

NOTES

....
....
....
....
....

Podcast Rating ⭐ ⭐ ⭐ ⭐ ⭐

Podcast name

....

EPISODE #

RECORDING DATE

PUBLISHING DATE

RECORDING LOCATION

TOPIC TO DISCUSS

....
....
....
....
....
....
....
....

HOSTS

GUESTS

LENGTH

MAIN GOAL FOR THIS PODCAST

....
....
....
....

CONTEST

SPONSOR ....
PRIZE ....
WINNER ....

TALKING POINTS

....
....
....
....
....
....

Podcast Review

THINGS I NEED TO PRACTICE

THINGS I REALLY ENJOYED :)

THINGS I DIDN'T EXPECTED

BUSINESS / PROMOTION

NOTES

Podcast Rating ☆ ☆ ☆ ☆ ☆

Podcast name

....

EPISODE

RECORDING DATE

PUBLISHING DATE

RECORDING LOCATION

TOPIC TO DISCUSS

....
....
....
....
....
....
....

HOSTS

GUESTS

LENGTH

MAIN GOAL FOR THIS PODCAST

....
....
....
....

CONTEST

SPONSOR ....
PRIZE ....
WINNER ....

TALKING POINTS

....
....
....
....
....
....

Podcast Review

THINGS I NEED TO PRACTICE

THINGS I REALLY ENJOYED :)

THINGS I DIDN'T EXPECTED

BUSINESS / PROMOTION

NOTES

Podcast Rating ☆ ☆ ☆ ☆ ☆

Podcast name

EPISODE

RECORDING DATE

PUBLISHING DATE

RECORDING LOCATION

TOPIC TO DISCUSS

HOSTS

GUESTS

LENGTH

MAIN GOAL FOR THIS PODCAST

CONTEST

SPONSOR

PRIZE

WINNER

TALKING POINTS

Podcast Review

THINGS I NEED TO PRACTICE

THINGS I REALLY ENJOYED :)

THINGS I DIDN'T EXPECTED

BUSINESS / PROMOTION

NOTES

Podcast Rating

Podcast name

....

EPISODE

RECORDING DATE

PUBLISHING DATE

RECORDING LOCATION

TOPIC TO DISCUSS

....
....
....
....
....
....
....

HOSTS

GUESTS

LENGTH

MAIN GOAL FOR THIS PODCAST

....
....
....
....

CONTEST

SPONSOR ....
PRIZE ....
WINNER ....

TALKING POINTS

....
....
....
....
....
....

Podcast Review

THINGS I NEED TO PRACTICE

THINGS I REALLY ENJOYED :)

THINGS I DIDN'T EXPECTED

BUSINESS / PROMOTION

NOTES

Podcast Rating ⭐ ⭐ ⭐ ⭐ ⭐

Podcast name

....

EPISODE #

RECORDING DATE

PUBLISHING DATE

RECORDING LOCATION

TOPIC TO DISCUSS

....
....
....
....
....
....
....

HOSTS

GUESTS

LENGTH

MAIN GOAL FOR THIS PODCAST

....
....
....
....

CONTEST

SPONSOR ....
PRIZE ....
WINNER ....

TALKING POINTS

....
....
....
....
....
....

Podcast Review

THINGS I NEED TO PRACTICE

THINGS I REALLY ENJOYED :)

THINGS I DIDN'T EXPECTED

BUSINESS / PROMOTION

NOTES

Podcast Rating ☆ ☆ ☆ ☆ ☆

Podcast name

....

EPISODE #

RECORDING DATE

PUBLISHING DATE

RECORDING LOCATION

TOPIC TO DISCUSS

....
....
....
....
....
....
....

HOSTS

GUESTS

LENGTH

MAIN GOAL FOR THIS PODCAST

....
....
....
....

CONTEST

SPONSOR ....
PRIZE ....
WINNER ....

TALKING POINTS

....
....
....
....
....
....

Podcast Review

THINGS I NEED TO PRACTICE

THINGS I REALLY ENJOYED :)

THINGS I DIDN'T EXPECTED

BUSINESS / PROMOTION

NOTES

Podcast Rating ☆ ☆ ☆ ☆ ☆

Podcast name

....

EPISODE #

RECORDING DATE

PUBLISHING DATE

RECORDING LOCATION

TOPIC TO DISCUSS

....
....
....
....
....
....
....

HOSTS

GUESTS

LENGTH

MAIN GOAL FOR THIS PODCAST

....
....
....
....

CONTEST

SPONSOR ....

PRIZE ....

WINNER ....

TALKING POINTS

....
....
....
....
....
....

Podcast Review

THINGS I NEED TO PRACTICE

THINGS I REALLY ENJOYED :)

THINGS I DIDN'T EXPECTED

BUSINESS / PROMOTION

NOTES

Podcast Rating

Podcast name ....

EPISODE

RECORDING DATE

PUBLISHING DATE

RECORDING LOCATION

TOPIC TO DISCUSS

....
....
....
....
....
....
....

HOSTS

GUESTS

LENGTH

MAIN GOAL FOR THIS PODCAST

....
....
....
....

CONTEST

SPONSOR ....
PRIZE ....
WINNER ....

TALKING POINTS

....
....
....
....
....
....

Podcast Review

THINGS I NEED TO PRACTICE

THINGS I REALLY ENJOYED :)

THINGS I DIDN'T EXPECTED

BUSINESS / PROMOTION

NOTES

Podcast Rating ☆ ☆ ☆ ☆ ☆

Podcast name

EPISODE

RECORDING DATE

PUBLISHING DATE

RECORDING LOCATION

TOPIC TO DISCUSS

HOSTS

GUESTS

LENGTH

MAIN GOAL FOR THIS PODCAST

CONTEST

SPONSOR

PRIZE

WINNER

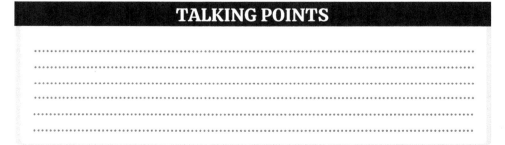

TALKING POINTS

Podcast Review

THINGS I NEED TO PRACTICE

THINGS I REALLY ENJOYED :)

THINGS I DIDN'T EXPECTED

BUSINESS / PROMOTION

NOTES

Podcast Rating ☆ ☆ ☆ ☆ ☆

Podcast name ....

EPISODE #

RECORDING DATE

PUBLISHING DATE

RECORDING LOCATION

TOPIC TO DISCUSS

....
....
....
....
....
....
....

HOSTS

GUESTS

LENGTH

MAIN GOAL FOR THIS PODCAST

....
....
....
....

CONTEST

SPONSOR ....
PRIZE ....
WINNER ....

TALKING POINTS

....
....
....
....
....
....

Podcast Review

THINGS I NEED TO PRACTICE

THINGS I REALLY ENJOYED :)

THINGS I DIDN'T EXPECTED

BUSINESS / PROMOTION

NOTES

Podcast Rating ⭐ ⭐ ⭐ ⭐ ⭐

Podcast name ....

EPISODE #	TOPIC TO DISCUSS

RECORDING DATE

PUBLISHING DATE

RECORDING LOCATION

HOSTS	GUESTS	LENGTH

MAIN GOAL FOR THIS PODCAST

CONTEST

SPONSOR ....

PRIZE ....

WINNER ....

TALKING POINTS

Podcast Review

THINGS I NEED TO PRACTICE

THINGS I REALLY ENJOYED :)

THINGS I DIDN'T EXPECTED

BUSINESS / PROMOTION

NOTES

Podcast Rating

Podcast name

....

EPISODE #

RECORDING DATE

PUBLISHING DATE

RECORDING LOCATION

TOPIC TO DISCUSS

....
....
....
....
....
....
....

HOSTS

GUESTS

LENGTH

MAIN GOAL FOR THIS PODCAST

....
....
....
....

CONTEST

SPONSOR ....
PRIZE ....
WINNER ....

TALKING POINTS

....
....
....
....
....
....

Podcast Review

THINGS I NEED TO PRACTICE

....
....
....
....

THINGS I REALLY ENJOYED :)

....
....
....
....

THINGS I DIDN'T EXPECTED

....
....
....
....

BUSINESS / PROMOTION

....
....
....
....
....

NOTES

....
....
....
....
....

Podcast Rating

⭐ ⭐ ⭐ ⭐ ⭐

Podcast name

....

EPISODE #

RECORDING DATE

PUBLISHING DATE

RECORDING LOCATION

TOPIC TO DISCUSS

....
....
....
....
....
....
....

HOSTS

GUESTS

LENGTH

MAIN GOAL FOR THIS PODCAST

....
....
....
....

CONTEST

SPONSOR ....
PRIZE ....
WINNER ....

TALKING POINTS

....
....
....
....
....
....

Podcast Review

THINGS I NEED TO PRACTICE

....
....
....
....

THINGS I REALLY ENJOYED :)

....
....
....
....

THINGS I DIDN'T EXPECTED

....
....
....
....

BUSINESS / PROMOTION

....
....
....
....
....

NOTES

....
....
....
....
....

Podcast Rating

☆ ☆ ☆ ☆ ☆

Podcast name

EPISODE #

RECORDING DATE

PUBLISHING DATE

RECORDING LOCATION

TOPIC TO DISCUSS

HOSTS

GUESTS

LENGTH

MAIN GOAL FOR THIS PODCAST

CONTEST

SPONSOR

PRIZE

WINNER

TALKING POINTS

Podcast Review

THINGS I NEED TO PRACTICE

....
....
....
....

THINGS I REALLY ENJOYED :)

....
....
....
....

THINGS I DIDN'T EXPECTED

....
....
....
....

BUSINESS / PROMOTION

....
....
....
....
....
....

NOTES

....
....
....
....
....
....

Podcast Rating ☆ ☆ ☆ ☆ ☆

Thank You!

so much for trying our Podcast Planner!
We'd love to hear from you!

If you've found this to be a good notebook please,
support us and leave a review.

Want free goodies?

If you have any suggestions or issues with this book, or if
you want to test some of our latest notebooks
please email us.

Send email to:

pickme.readme@gmail.com